Matthew 19:14 (KJNV)
But Jesus said, "Let the little children come to Me, and do not forbid them; for of such is the kingdom of heaven."

What has been written is based on real events, each experience with a little twist. The outcome is exactly how it was.

Saving a King

Chapter 1 – King barks for help 2

Chapter 2 – King tames Max 8

Chapter 3 – Nana and the apple cores 13

Chapter 4 – Fun at the Beach 17

Chapter 5 – Waterbugs and Dragonflies 22

Chapter 6 – Learning how to Iron 24

Chapter 7 – Sunday School and Meringue Pie 27

Chapter 8 – Tadpoles and Frogs 33

Chapter 9 – King is now a Prince 36

Chapter 10 – My Prayers are answered 38

Chapter 1 – King barks for help

It was the start of the Christmas holidays, and we had eight lovely weeks to enjoy the long hot, Australian summer, with no schoolbooks or teachers in sight! The first day started off perfectly, and the sun shining on the bedroom window was calling me out to play.

First, there were the morning chores to get through; making my bed and putting away our toys and games that we had left out from the night before. Then it was time to hurry down some breakfast, get the dishes done, and race outside onto my bike, ready to ride off on our first holiday adventure. I was early though, and I thought I could surprise Mum by vacuuming the carpets too. I grabbed the cleaner and plugged it in, thinking how happy Mum would be when she saw the clean carpets.

"*Oh no!*" I couldn't believe it when dust and fluff went flying everywhere, also filling my mouth, making me cough and splutter. I moaned loudly when I saw that I had put the hose in the wrong end of the vacuum cleaner. Not only were there dusty bits of fluff all over me, but there was dust and fluff all over the kitchen. My Mum had lived in an orphanage from when she was young, and they were extremely strict with the kids, so she was extremely strict, too. We had to keep the house like a new packet of pins, otherwise I would hear her calling out my name like "Maaareeey!"

I had long, curly red hair that was always tangled, with pale skin that liked to freckle. I was nicknamed "Sarah," after a famous actress (Sarah Bernhardt), and Mum said I was acting all the time. I knew I was a daydreamer and often clumsy, falling over things for no reason, plus I had nightmares and walked in my sleep, and had found myself waking up in strange places, like my brothers' wardrobe in the middle of the night or climbing through the bedroom window.

My Mum said I had an active imagination and daydreamed too much, and the teacher's loved writing on my report cards from school that I was easily distracted. Who wouldn't want to stare out the window, watching the birds play in the trees, or watch the other kids running around the play area?

There was no use daydreaming now, I *had* to clean up the kitchen again, and that meant putting the hose in the *right* end of the vacuum cleaner and cleaning the floor, *plus* I needed to dust everything in the room as well. I knew I shouldn't be upset about having to clean up this mess; it was my fault for being in such a hurry, but I did feel a bit annoyed at myself for not concentrating on what I was doing. Thankfully, once I started cleaning the time went fast and finally, everything was back to normal. I did manage a quick laugh when I saw myself in the mirror; all I could see was my eyes and mouth, the rest was dusty bits of fluff. I had a quick shower and threw clean clothes on.

Soon I was riding my bike out of the gates, and heading off to our meeting place, laughing to myself with holiday happiness. We usually met at the abandoned church, which also had an old, no longer used cemetery behind it, making it an awesomely spooky place to catch up. We often walked around the cemetery, talking about the old falling down graves, and wondering what had happened to the people buried there. A few old grape vines grew at the back of the cemetery and every year it grew big, beautiful purple grapes. Alongside the vines was an old mulberry tree, and not only was it perfect to climb, but we could also eat delicious mulberries to our hearts' content. We were always covered in purple juice when we climbed down with our little buckets of mulberries to take home.

The church was across the road and a couple of blocks away from where we lived, and it was also surrounded by magnificent climbing trees that reached the top of the church steeple. We all loved to climb as high as we could and look down on the old cemetery, sitting up there telling spooky ghost stories, trying to scare each other.

My home was the closest to the church, and I could see there was a group of kids waiting there already. I could see my best friend Heather, riding her bike flat out and nearly at my place. I yelled out "Hurry up, Heather" and I could see her legs pumping a bit faster.

Heather and I we were opposites – she had short blonde hair with tanned skin, and where I was a daydreamer and often clumsy, Heather was more alert and aware of what was going on. I think that is why we were such good friends. When Heather reached us, we all laughed with holiday excitement and had a quick discussion on where we should go. We all agreed to catch tadpoles, and that meant going to the *big* drain.

Running alongside the church was the drain, and the adults said it was out of bounds to us. We heard that the drain was occupied by giant, slimy, water rats with big dirty teeth, but none of us had ever seen any. We thought the scary stories had been made up by our parents, trying to scare us enough to keep us away from the drain. If luck was on our side, there would be no-one around and we could leave our bikes on the side of the drain and jump the few feet down to the bottom to go and catch some tadpoles.

There was nothing more exciting than watching the miracle of tadpoles turning into frogs, losing their long tails, gaining legs, and getting a whole new look. They went from needing to swim all the time to being able to sit on the rocks and enjoy the sun on their faces, and then those frogs would disappear. They would join up with the other frogs from previous summers, singing and croaking all through the night. I think watching tadpoles evolve was one of the miracles God wanted to show us, so we could learn about changing into new ways of life.

Listening to the croaks of all the frogs we had gathered over the years was like summer music, when we were sleeping outside, trying to keep cool from the heat. We all thought the more frogs singing the merrier! They sang through the day too, although I don't think Mum liked them singing as much as we did, while she was hanging the clothes on the line.

The boys were always well prepared when we went hunting for tadpoles – they had a coat hanger twisted into a loop with one of their Mum's stockings forced over the loop, making a great strainer. They had brought their big glass jars with lids that had holes punched into them, letting the air through so the tadpoles could breathe.

Luck was on our side and there were no adults around, either in the church or near the drain, so we rode through the gates and over to the fence. We all jumped from our bikes, leaving them lying on their sides, hiding them behind the bushes. We climbed over the fence, jumping down into the drain. There wasn't much water along the middle and none on the sides, so we had plenty of room to run without getting our feet wet.

We got to the usual spot where the tadpoles were, which was a rocky, watery join in the drain. We were ready to start swirling the nets around when we noticed a beautiful golden Labrador further up the drain. The dog barked at us, then ran further ahead, and of course, we were off on another great adventure! "Hey, wait for us" we called out as we went chasing the dog, who kept on outrunning us. The dog would stop, turn around and bark at us until we almost caught up, and then it was off running away again. This went on for a while, and we were getting very hot and thirsty, but we were sure the dog was leading us to something exciting, so we kept on following.

Eventually the dog stopped running and he was as exhausted as we were. Once he became used to us, he was very friendly - trusting us and showing this by giving each of us a big licking. He was beautiful but had no collar or name tag and after loudly calling out different ideas for a name, we decided to call him King. King didn't lead us to anything real exciting, so we decided we needed to take him home with us, not knowing what else we could do. There was no-one else in our group that would be able to keep King at home, so I bravely said that my Mum would let me keep him.

Now I had to talk Mum into letting him stay and I said a little prayer to myself; "Dear God, please make Mum let me keep King forever, and I'll be extra good for as long as I can. And thank you for giving us pets to love. Amen."

We got King to stay with us as we picked up our bikes and crossed the road to my home. He was very thirsty, and we thought he was probably dirty too, so we gave him an outside bath. I used the shampoo that was in the bathroom, then grabbed some towels and we took turns drying him off. King was quite happy and relaxed as we took care of him, and he did look very special with his beautiful brown eyes and glorious golden fur.

My Mum was due home from work in a couple of hours, so we added up how much pocket money we had as we had decided King needed a collar and lead. I locked him in my bedroom, and we all rode off to the pet store, which was on the main road. This meant we had to ride past the deli that sold the broken biscuits cheap, but I wouldn't use my money until we had what King needed. We had to go past the house with the fig tree with branches hanging over the fence, so we decided to grab figs instead.

The owners didn't mind, and they told us they had too many and were happy for us to eat them. "These are the best figs ever" I called out, and I would remember to thank God for giving us fruit when I said my Prayers that night. We had enough money between us to buy a black leather collar and a chain lead, some dog food, a water bowl, and we *still* had change left over to buy some broken biscuits on the way home. The shop sold the biscuits that were broken to us much cheaper than the biscuits that were perfect.

When we got to the shop, we bought a big bottle of fizzy drink as well as the biscuits to share. We ended up taking much longer than expected and I realized Mum would be home already, and King was locked in my bedroom. We took off for home and rode as fast as we could, but as we went through the back gate, I could see Mum's bike and knew she was home.

Chapter 2 – King tames Max

I had that awful, sinking gut feeling when something is wrong, so I told the others they better go home and I'll explain to Mum about King on my own, as I thought it would be better that way. We would catch up again in the morning at our meeting spot as I was sure I would be grounded for the rest of the day. I quietly crept inside but Mum was waiting for me, and I heard her call out "Maaareeey, come here."

Not only was I in trouble for having King locked in my room (luckily, he just slept and didn't make a mess, but had decided my sister Carol's bed was the best), I had also used her good shampoo, and they were her good towels that I had tossed on the laundry floor. I *knew* I wouldn't do that again. There was still fluff and dust all through the kitchen and on top of the fridge and cupboards that I hadn't seen.

I put on my best acting voice and pleaded with Mum to let me keep King; "Please, please Mum, let me keep him" and I softened my eyes, so they were begging too. After hearing my explanation on how I wanted to surprise her by doing the vacuuming, Mum could see my intentions were good, and she forgave me for making such a mess. Luckily, she had fallen in love with King too, while she was waiting for me to come home. She also forgave me for locking him in my bedroom, and using her good towels, but I don't think she was incredibly happy that I had used her best shampoo to wash King. "No wonder he looks so shiny, that's very expensive shampoo!" she said, after I told her that everyone said he was handsome and shiny. She said a few more words about being me needing to be responsible and growing up, and I knew I would never do that again!"

Mum thankfully agreed that we could keep King, but we would have to check the newspapers a daily to see if anyone put an ad in for a lost dog. I had to be happy with that, and we both cleaned up the dust and fluff that I hadn't noticed before. I promised not to use the good towels for King, and I made an extra special promise not to use her good shampoo again. I gave her a big happy hug, put the lead and chain on King and went happily skipping down the street. I was looking for anyone I could find to admire King, and Mum likes us playing outside in the fresh air.

King was a big hit with the neighbours and the kids around the block, and he would sit and shake hands on command. The two young dancing twins, Rachael, and Hilary loved him so much already, that they wanted to walk him by themselves. "Please, please" they begged, and as he was so easy to walk, and so well behaved, I knew he would be okay with them. They skipped along the footpath, still in their dancing costumes, sparkling in the sun, with King looking so clean and handsome that my heart just warmly melted. I laughed softly to myself, thinking this was the best start ever to the school holidays.

We rounded up a few kids, then went and played chasey in the local park, with King running around chasing us as well. We were all so happy, running around until the sun started to set, and it was time to head home. There were big black clouds gathering in the sky, and we knew there was going to be a massive storm. We loved seeing the flash of lightning and then counting until we heard the thunder, telling us how many miles away the storm was.

I wanted King to sleep on my bed, but as I shared the room with two sisters (my brother had his own room), they had to agree first. My eldest sister had said "no way" and didn't want King in the room with us, so we made up a bed up for him in the lounge room, under the splendid Christmas tree that we had put up last week.

When I said my prayers that night, I said a special thanks to God for giving me King, and I remembered to add another special thanks for fruit. We always started with "Now I lay me down to sleep, I pray the Lord my soul to keep; Guide me, Jesus, through the night and wake me with the morning light" and then added the new things for which we were thankful. We always finished with Amen

I heard a big crash of thunder that woke me up, then I saw the next flash of lightning and as I lay there, I started to count and got to nine before the thunder roared above. The storm was still nine miles away, and heading in our direction, so I knew it was going to be a big one. We had learned that you count once you see the lightening, and then stop when you heard the thunder, and this told us how many miles away the storm was.

I could hear a whimpering sound, and realized it was King crying in the lounge room. I rushed in to see him, and he was so scared that I got my pillow and quilt and made a bed up under the Christmas tree next to him. We cuddled up together and I whispered to him "It's okay King, I'm here to look after you." He wasn't as frightened when the storm continued to roar and crash around us, and he didn't whimper again, and it wasn't very long before we both fell asleep.

When we woke up in the morning, I took King out to the back yard and made sure the gate was closed. We had three bantams, Max the rooster and two hens; the black one was Alice, and the speckled one was Ethyl. They were so cute as babies, but Max grew up loving to peck hard at our ankles, and we learned how to race through the yard and back inside before he could get in a good peck with his sharp beak. I slowly led King into the back section, which the chooks also used, to see if they all got along together, with no pecking from Max. King was happy playing with the chooks, and they weren't scared of him at all and Max didn't peck at King, which really amazed me.

I left King with the chooks, giving me a chance to get my chores done, so I could get ready for another day of no school, playing with my friends in the sunshine! We also had King to play with, making the day even more perfect. I had to be home for lunch though, as my Nana was coming for a visit, and I hadn't seen her for a long time. I knew Mum wasn't all that happy about her coming to visit, but I was excited. My Mum and her brothers were separated after my grandfather died, when Mum was five. She was the oldest and Mum went to an orphanage for girls, and her brothers all went to an orphanage for boys. I knew they had been separated when they were still young children, but I didn't know the whole story.

We gathered at the church again and climbed onto the roof, looking down over the cemetery, telling more spooky stories. Luckily, there was a gate that we could shut to keep King in, and we laughed as we watched him trying to climb the tree to get up to us. After a while, we decided to play 'Red Rover All Over,' a game of skill involving running across the oval, on an area we marked out, trying to get to the other side without being caught by the one in the middle. It could be a bit rough though, and sometimes we would hit the ground with a nice old thud.

We remembered that Robert had broken his ankle last summer, and the doctor told him he couldn't go swimming with a cast on, so we were all trying to make sure we didn't break any bones. None of us wanted to wear a cast during summer, winter wouldn't be as bad! King was happily chasing all of us and didn't know the rules, so we were all catching each other, trying to dodge him. There was so much loud laughter that in the end, there really was no winner, except for King. He just kept on making us love him more as we got to know him better.

When we had enough of 'Red Rover' we decided to go to the playground, and we all jumped on a piece of equipment. Everyone always wanted the swings, so that is where they all raced off to, but I went to the see-saw instead, and Evelyn came with me. Heather managed to get a swing, and those who were waiting their turn decided to give her an extra boost, sending her higher than the top of the bar holding up the swing. Heather went hurtling over the top, and she was flung off, flying really high, and then she landed with a thud as she hit the ground, along with the loud snap of a bone breaking. We knew that sound from when Robert broke his ankle, but at least he had gotten through some of the summer holidays.

"*Owwww*" Heather sat up yelling loudly and crying out aloud in pain, and we could see it was her wrist that she had broken. Luckily, it was her left wrist, and she was right-handed, but I don't think she felt very lucky right then. We managed to get Heather to sit on the bar of one of the bikes and we wheeled her out of the playground, but she was crying out in pain. We must have looked a bit strange to Heather's neighbour that just happened to be driving past, and she pulled over to see if everything was all right.

We were all yelling out at the same time what had happened, and when she saw Heather's wrist, she decided to take Heather home in her car, and then ring her mother so she could go to the hospital. We waved sadly to Heather as they were driving off, and we all felt sad that she would have to wear a cast in summer. We would enjoy writing messages and drawing all over her cast though, and we'd make get well cards, too. We had done this for Robert last summer, and it had cheered him up.

It was close to lunch time, so I took King home and decided to try and teach him some more tricks until Nana came, and we worked on 'lie down.' He had a bag of little treats for rewards, and each time he would lie down, I would give him a treat. King worked this trick out in a flash, so I started on getting him to lie down and then roll over. King was very clever, and we had a lot of fun with these new tricks. I was having so much fun that I forgot to eat my own lunch and life was perfect.

Chapter 3 – Nana and the apple cores

There was a knock on the door, and I let my Nana in; she was tall and had lovely silver-gray hair and she gave me a big hug, and I told her I was Mary. Nana had a happy smile, and she smelled nice too, like a forest in Heaven. It was lovely seeing her, and I was so glad King was there with us. She could watch all the new tricks I had been teaching him. Nana had brought two cans of baby food with her as she thought my younger sister and I were still toddlers. I thought I would heat one can up and I chose the chicken and vegetables, which would be perfect for lunch. My younger sister Lynne could have the chocolate custard when she got home from her friend's house.

Baby rice was delicious, and we had that often, so I thought that the chicken and vegetables would be, too. While the can was boiling, I was telling Nana I was really hungry as I'd forgotten to eat lunch, and then Nana took the can out of the boiling water and burnt her fingers trying to open it. Her fingers weren't too bad, and once she opened it, she poured it into a little bowl. It smelt all right, but when I took the first mouthful, I nearly spat it out. It was nothing like I expected, and I felt sorry for the babies that had to eat that food. I did manage to swallow it and looked at what was still in the bowl, and although the can was only little, it looked as if there was a heck of a lot still to eat.

I forced down the rest because I didn't want to hurt Nana's feelings and hoped I didn't pull too many faces while I was swallowing each mouthful. I can't even think of what this baby food tasted like, but I really didn't like brussel sprouts, and eating that food was almost as bad as those sprouts. I made Nana a cup of tea, showing her how grown up I was, and I quickly drank 2 glasses of water to wash down the taste of the baby food. I told Nana I was very thirsty.

Then it was time to show off King and his tricks, and Nana told King he was the cleverest dog she knew. We played with King for a while, giving him lots of hugs and cuddles, then Nana wanted to walk to the big shops to buy some things. We decided to leave King home as they didn't allow dogs in the shops, so I locked him in with the chooks again.

We went for our walk and went into the supermarket first, and then we went to the grocery store for some Granny Smith apples. Nana wanted to go into the deli to buy us each a drink, and Nana said to leave the bag of apples outside the deli. She leant them against the wall, and I told her it wasn't a good idea, someone would steal them, but Nana thought they would be safe there. When we left the shop with our drinks, the bag of apples was gone. I felt really sorry for Nana but as we walked a bit further, I saw the first apple core and I called out "Nana –

look!" and then we saw another apple core and then another. We both started laughing aloud and Nana said, "at least the apples were eaten."

We walked slowly home, and Nana was asking about my school and friends, and I asked Nana about her life, too. Her name was Frances and she lived in a retirement village and had lots of friends, but she missed all of us. She was going to stay overnight and would be sleeping in my brother Steve's room, and we would have a night of playing cards and board games. Mum was due home soon, and she would be bringing the paper to check for lost dogs. I said a silent prayer; "Oh, please God, don't let there be any ads for King in the paper and I'll keep on being extra good. I'll even eat more baby food if Nana brings it again. Amen."

King rushed to the fence when Nana and I got home and he started jumping around, trying to lick us both. King and I had learned to love each other very quickly and although King didn't mind staying in with the chooks when I went out, he was always really excited when I got home. He didn't chase the chooks but was very nosey, making me laugh when he was trying to work out what the chooks were doing, as they scratched around in their yard. He would tilt his head from side to side, as if he could get a better look, and there was a question in his big, soft golden-brown eyes.

Mum came home, then my brother Steve and my younger sister Lynne, but my eldest sister Carol was spending a few nights of the holidays at her friend's home. We had such big age gaps that we all had our own group of friends and hobbies, although we had our evenings together and loved playing games and going to the beach or the public swimming pools. We all made a fuss of Nana, and then my sister tried her baby food, but she didn't like it either and didn't even finish hers. I really wished I had chosen the chocolate one, it smelt really nice, so I had a taste and then finished it off. It was actually quite nice!

Mum didn't say anything about an ad in the paper for a lost dog, so I didn't bring it up in case she had forgotten to check. We got excited because Mum had brought home fish and chips, which we would eat from paper plates, then we would have ice cream and fruit for dessert. We had bread, butter, and sauce so that we could make sandwiches if we felt like it, and it was just like having an indoor picnic. It was a special night for all of us, and I'm sure I saw happy tears in Nana's eyes.

We all cleared the table and then we had our dessert, which was perfect for a summer evening and a night for playing cards. It didn't take long to do the dishes, and soon we were all sitting back at the table again, this time with cards. We had decided to play 'Go Fish' and we all got noisy as we called out the cards for which we were fishing. We decided to play some very noisy games of 'Cheat' and Lynne ended up overall winner for the night. I'm fairly sure the adults had something to do with letting the youngest one win, but no one cared, we just had a great night with a lot of laughter.

Soon it was time for bed, and luckily enough, King was able to sleep on my bed as my eldest sister wasn't home, and she wouldn't know he was sleeping in our room. I thanked God for King again in my prayers as well as praying to keep us all safe. King snuggled up behind my knees and we had a perfect sleep, sweetly dreaming together. I knew King was dreaming because his legs were running in his sleep, and he was making little happy sounds. I'm sure it was about chasing balls and having fun.

It seemed like I had been asleep for a few minutes and then it was time to get up and start another glorious school holiday day. We got up early to see Nana off and after a lot of hugs and a few tears, her taxi drove off and we were waving goodbye. I knew that Mum and Nana had sorted out their problems, and Mum was sad to see Nana go, too.

Chapter 4 – Fun at the Beach

Dad was home from work for a few days – he was a train driver and often away for a week or so at a time and today he had promised to take us to the beach the next morning. I loved having Dad home from work; he was always whistling, and he was so tall and muscly. His friends would come and visit too and bring their wives and kids. We would all play chasey at the playground and oval, or cards if it was dark, Dad called me Angles, his way of saying angel. I loved that nickname too. We would always have fish and chips those nights, which was another thing I loved about Dad being home.

I could take one friend to the beach with me, and I chose to take Heather as she had broken her wrist, which was now in a cast. I walked King to Heather's home, and when she came to the door, I yelled out with excitement; "Heather, Dad said you can come to the beach with us. Tell your Mum we will make sure your plaster stays dry and ask if you can stay the night. Dad said we'll leave early in the morning." Heather's Mum said it was okay, and we needed to make sure the cast stayed dry. We left King in her backyard while Heather packed her bathers and pajamas and clothes to change into. We were so happy walking back to my place, and we sang while we walked. We stopped a couple of times to draw beautiful ladies on the footpath with the sticks we found along the way. Heather could still draw, but I know her wrist was still painful, even though she was making out it didn't hurt anymore.

My sister was still away, and King slept on my bed and Heather slept in Carols' bed. When we had finished breakfast and cleaning up, we loaded our tent, picnic lunch, towels, and hats, and off we went. The beach we were going to had side shows with rides and swings; we were so excited and couldn't wait to get there.

Heather's plaster had plenty of drawings and names written all over it and it was very impressive, although she had to keep it dry when we went into the water. No swimming for her, but at least she could wade around in the shallow water and go on the rides, enjoying the sunny day that was perfect for playing at the beach. We had to leave King behind as we didn't have enough room in the car for him, but he seemed happy enough playing with the chickens and Max never chased him at all. We all wished Max wouldn't chase us but perhaps he enjoyed seeing us running away and yelling out to stop him from pecking our ankles.

Dad set up our tent and laid out the blanket, making sure our Esky was in the shade with our food and cold drinks, and we put our little foam surf boards next to the tent ready for when we headed into the water. We decided to go onto the rides first, and Heather and I went on the Gee Whiz, which was a super-fast ride that also spun around in the air. Heather was finding it hard to hang on, using only her right hand and she started screaming, and next thing, I was screaming with her. We must have made lots of noise because I could see Dad frantically waving his arms around, and then the man that was operating the ride slowed it right down until stopped so that we could both get off. Once we were safely back on the ground, Dad gave us both a hug and we felt a bit silly, wishing we had stayed on until the end, but then we watched my brother on his ride.

Steve decided to go on the Octopus, which was higher and faster than the ride we went on, and somehow, he forgot to pull down the safety bar. We were sure Steve was going to be thrown off, but he managed to stay on as he was flung from one side of the carriage to the other, and he sat through the whole ride, without even one scream. Even though it had been a bit scary watching him, and Dad was sort of freaking out, when he got off the ride, we laughed and teased him about forgetting to pull down the safety bar. He didn't think it was funny at all and so he started teasing us for screaming and making them stop our ride. I guess shutting down the Gee Whiz for everyone else did earn us medals for being the most scared kids, so we didn't really say much more about it after that.

Dad decided it was time for us to have our lunch and then he bought us all an ice cream and we played in the sand for a while. I don't think he wanted us on anymore rides and he thought eating ice cream and playing in the sand was safer, or at least, quieter. We built a great moat running from the edge of the water, with a magnificent sandcastle in the middle.

The moat filled up a bit and then we added shells and seaweed, and we played around in the shallow water so Heather could keep her plaster dry. My brother Steve decided to jump right into the middle of our castle, flattening it so that it was just a lump of wet sand, with our shells scattered through the sand. Heather and I yelled at him for ruining our castle, and he said we had embarrassed him when we laughed at him for not pulling the safety bar down, and he was paying us back.

I really did need to learn more about brothers! Looking at the flattened sandcastle reminded me of one of my favourite songs that we sang at Sunday School, "The Wise Man Built His House Upon the Rocks." The rain came down and the floods came up, and the wise man's house stood firm. Heather and I decided the water was going to sink the castle anyway, and rather than getting upset, we would go and do something else. This made Dad happier too, as he didn't really like hearing us yelling and arguing. He told us we were embarrassing him, and people were looking at us, but we couldn't see anyone looking our way. He just wanted us to be quiet.

We had been to learn to swim lessons with the school, so we could all swim, but we didn't want to leave Heather by herself in the shallow water, so we all stayed in the warm, shallow water with her. After a while, playing in the shallow water was boring, so we decided we could sit Heather on one of the surf boards so that she could go out a little bit deeper, but we should have known this wasn't a good plan. She did manage to keep her balance until a bigger wave came and sent her flying off the little surfboard. Luckily, we were in the sun and her cast wasn't in the water too long and dried quickly, so apart from the smudged messages and drawings, all ended well.

It seemed like no time had passed, and it was time to leave, so we had to shake the sand off everything and pack up. We washed the sand from our feet and climbed into the car and headed home. It had been an awesome day out, but at least I had King waiting for me when I got home, so I didn't feel too sad about leaving the beach. We dropped Heather off first and then went home. I rushed to the backyard and let King out and he was jumping all around and licking me with happiness and making happy yelping sounds and I quickly thought "Thank you, God, for sending me King" and then we went inside.

It was still daylight, so I took King, and we walked around the corner and found some friends playing hopscotch. We decided to go to the playground again, and no-one pushed the swing so high that it flipped over, and there was no accident or broken bones. King was happy chasing us and he loved running around the oval and rolling on the grass, and we were all happily playing. It was soon time to go home though, and I knew Mum would be there with the paper, checking to see if there was any ad for a lost dog. Nothing had been said for a long time, and although I didn't ask, I knew there had been no ads, or Mum would have told me.

After dinner we decided to put the TV on the front verandah and sit outside as it was still hot inside, and our neighbours came and joined us. Rodney and Deborah lived on one side of the house, and although they were younger than us, we still managed to play hide and seek, but King kept giving our hiding spots away. We stayed outside until the neighbours went home, and then we took the TV back inside and it was time for bed. Sometimes it was so hot inside that we all slept outside, and we would build a tent on the clothesline, made from our spare blankets pegged to the outside line.

These were the nights when we could really hear our frogs singing, and we would look for the different stars; the Saucepan, the Milky Way and the Southern Cross were our favorites to find, probably as they were the easiest. There is nothing like the night sky when it's dark and just the moon and the stars are giving us light. Our parents might let us have a tent night tomorrow night. King was going to sleep on my bed again so after I had said my prayers, he snuggled up behind my knees and then we were both dreaming happily.

Chapter 5 – Waterbugs and Dragonflies

It was Friday already and near the end of the first week of school holidays. We had the usual morning; and King was in with the chooks while I got my chores done and ate my breakfast. I spent some time with King on a new trick; this time I was getting him to turn around in a circle, and then it was time to meet my friends. Heather wasn't there as she struggled riding her bike with her broken wrist, but there was a nice group of 7, so we climbed to the top of the old church while we worked out what we would do for the day.

We decided on a longer ride and a picnic lunch, so we all went in our different directions and organised our own lunches. I made a Vegemite sandwich, and we had watermelon in the fridge, so I cut a thick slice, and I packed some treats for King. We needed water, so I filled a small esky container and grabbed King's water bowl. It all fitted neatly into the little basket on the front of my bike, and King happily ran alongside me on his lead and our little group met at the old church again.

We went to the playground that was near the lake, and not too far to ride. King didn't care where we went, he was simply happy being with us, but he did love the little lake. After running around it a few times, he ended up walking in and splashing around, really enjoying himself. We were laughing at him and his silly antics when we all noticed a dragonfly hovering just above the water. This reminded me of the story of the waterbugs and the dragonfly I had learned at Sunday School. We were sitting around in a group, watching King and the dragonfly, so I told the story as I remembered it.

"The waterbugs lived at the bottom of the lake; they were a happy bunch and loved their friends. However, every now and then one of them would float to the surface of the pond, and never return. This saddened the waterbugs left behind as they missed their friends that kept leaving them, and they tried to swim to the top of the lake to follow their friends, but they could not get to the top, no matter how they tried! All the waterbugs got together and made a pact that the next one to float up to the top of the pond would come back and tell the waterbugs left behind where they went, when they reached the surface of the lake.

The next waterbug was floating to the top, and lo and behold, when he reached the top, he had evolved into a glorious dragonfly. Oh, how he loved his marvelous wings, and he soared here, and he soared there, looking down on the trees, the flowers, and the grass; he especially loved the sunshine and delighted in his new life. Finally, he remembered his pact to the other waterbugs, and he soared down at the water and bounced off.

He soared down at the water harder and then harder, trying to get back down to see his waterbug friends, but he kept bouncing back. He was so excited about the new world he was living in and disappointed that he couldn't get to see his friends again. "It doesn't matter" he thought, "they will soon follow me and float to the top. Then they will marvel at their own new lives, loving their wings and soaring and flying in the sunshine!" So, next time *you* see a dragonfly hovering above the water, you will know he is thinking of his waterbug friends!

I thought that waterbugs and dragonflies were another way God was teaching us about the miracles of life, and how we can all end up with wings, soaring around like the dragonfly or flying more gently, like the butterfly.

Time flies by so quickly when you are having fun, and before long it was time to put King back on his lead and pack our things back into our baskets, and head home. King dried on the way, but I was thinking he might need another bath after playing in the lake. I would have to buy special pet shampoo and not use my mothers like I did last time. I had already spent my pocket money, so we would have to wait until Monday.

Chapter 6 – Learning how to Iron

I played basketball on Saturdays at the Sunday School with my friend Joanne, and she would be at my home early as she didn't have a bike, and we had a long walk to get to the church. We didn't care as we sang songs like "There was an old man named Michael Finnegan, he grew whiskers on his chinnegan, the wind came down and blew them in again, poor old Michael Finnegan; begin again," or "On top of spaghetti, all covered in cheese, I lost my poor meatball, when somebody sneezed. It rolled on the table and onto the floor, and then my poor meatball rolled out of the door."

I had put King in with the chooks again, but Mum said she might let him out to have a play inside and I knew she was falling in love with him, too. He would be safe until I got home, so we just had fun on the way there and then it was time to play basketball. I played in the centre, and I was always nervous before we started playing but once the whistle blew, I forgot about my nerves and just concentrated on getting the ball out of the centre and down to our goal end.

Joanne was one of our goalies, and she was playing a really great game, which got the rest of the team fired up, and we were flying after the ball, our shoes sliding on the court. We were all accurate with the goals that day, and we won the game. At the end of every game each team stood in a circle and sang out "three cheers for the umpire" and we all shook each other's hands. We didn't always win, but we always had fun and they gave us oranges at half time, and plenty of water to drink. At the end of each season, the umpires voted for the best and fairest player to teach us it wasn't about winning or losing but being a good sport.

Before long we were heading back home again, and this time we were singing "Old McDonald had a farm" and "The Grand Old Duke of York" as they sounded like winning songs. We drew pictures of ladies in the gravel on the footpath and tried to work out which drawing was the best, but we always liked our own. We thought they were beautiful, elegant women with long ball gowns and jewels and long flowing hair, like Cinderella. Well, at least *we* thought they were beautiful drawings, not just lines in the dust.

I always went with Mum to the shops on Saturday afternoon, after we had eaten our lunch, so I didn't get much chance to play with King before we were heading off again. He did seem to enjoy his time with the chooks, and I never saw Max try to peck at him, although he still tried to peck my ankle if I ever went into their chook yard. I thought he was a cranky old rooster, but he was beautiful, with shiny peacock blue feathers on his tail and a sort of orange colour on his wings. He held his head straight up in the air and you could see he was proud looking after Ethyl and Alice. Ethyl was perfectly speckled, and Alice was black and shone in the sunlight. They made such a cute family and King just added something special to their little chook-house, although he never slept in their roosting boxes.

When we were home from shopping and we had packed it all away, Mum sat down to read the paper and I was dreading her finding an ad for a lost dog, but once again there was no ad. I was so thankful I said another prayer of thanks to God, and then it was time to take King out for a run and find out who was ready to play. Before that though, I thought I would help Mum out and iron our Sunday School clothes, ready for the morning. I set up the ironing board and grabbed the first thing that needed ironing, which happened to be my brother's shirt.

It was meant to be a surprise, but I was the one that got the surprise when I put the iron to the shirt and a great hunk of shirt stuck to the iron, leaving a massive hole. "Oh no," I had ruined it! Now I had to explain to my Mum what I had done and was praying that she wouldn't be too upset, and that I could still take King out to play. Mum wasn't really impressed with my ironing efforts when I showed her the ruined shirt, and she showed me how to clean the stuck shirt from the iron and explained about the heat settings and how to read the labels so that I wouldn't do it again. Of course, it was my brother's favourite shirt, so I knew he wouldn't be too happy with me.

Mum said it was okay for me to go outside and play, and I really think she was happy to see me heading out the door. King and I walked around the corner to find out which of our friends were still at home. It turned out that there were a few of us, so we decided to head over to the old church again and climb a couple of the tall trees that we loved so much. There was nothing quite like looking out over the roofs of the houses and seeing all the gardens and people walking around, doing their gardening, or just relaxing in the glorious summer sun.

We sat up there for a while, and then decided we would take King into the playground and let him run around while we played on the swings and things. We played chasey and red rover all over and next thing we knew it was time to go home to our dinner. We made our plans to get together after dinner for an hour or so; it was Saturday night, and they were special at our home.

Chapter 7 – Sunday School and Meringue Pie

Whenever Dad was home on a Saturday night, he would bring a big bag of lollies to share and soft drinks for us, too, so we stayed up later than normal. I used to like watching the beginning of the Saturday night movie, but when that was over it was time for bed. That night Dad had fallen asleep on the floor watching TV, and we could hear him snoring, so we crept back out of bed to watch some more TV. Each time Dad rolled over or stopped snoring, we would rush back to bed until we heard his snores again. I'm pretty sure Dad knew that we sneaked around him when he was sleeping on the floor and was silently laughing each time we went running out the door. We had a lot of experience from previous Saturday nights.

The next morning, it was time for Sunday School and Mum tied a five-cent piece into our hankies so we wouldn't lose it. Sunday School was earlier than church, so she would meet us there later and bring Lynne, so Carol, Steve and I rode our bikes. Mum always dressed me just before we were leaving to go anywhere, so I wouldn't get dirty before we left. The reason she did this was when I was little and loved sitting in the puddle at the end of the driveway, getting my good clothes wet and muddy. I listened to that excuse every time *we* were running late, and *I* was getting more tempted to ask, *"why didn't you just fill in the hole in the driveway?,"* but it wasn't normally the right time for that question. So, we were running late again, and Carol and Steve were waiting for me.

We always stopped at the shop on the way and bought some broken biscuits, so we had the change for the collection plates. We also like to pick a couple of the figs hanging over the fence on the way, so they wanted to leave early. Anyway, we had time to get our biscuits, eat our figs and before long we were sitting in Sunday School, and I was colouring in.

The Scripture of the day was Matthew 19:14 But Jesus said, "Let the little children come to me. Don't stop them, because the kingdom of heaven belongs to people who are like these children." The picture we were colouring in was beautiful, it showed Jesus holding a little lamb, with children happily playing all around him, and it gave us such a well-loved, peaceful feeling.

I was in a younger class than Carol and Steve; they were in the Youth Group, and I really hoped their Scripture was just as beautiful. We used drawings for scriptures to colour in, as it was easier for us to understand. The song we sang as we were learning was "Jesus loves the little children, all the children of the world. Red, brown, yellow, black, and white, they are precious in his sight, Jesus loves the little children of the world." I didn't stay for the church sermon as I was too young, but our class could go outside and practice basketball or skipping and there was a hopscotch game painted on the asphalt.

I knew Mum was having visitors for lunch, and when the service was over and she was chatting with her friends, I asked if I could go home early and play with King. It was okay if I remembered to change out of my good clothes and into play clothes. Riding home I was singing the song "Sing a Song of Sixpence" and when I got to the words "now wasn't that a dainty dish to set before a king?" and it reminded me of *my* King, waiting with the chooks until I got home, and we would go out and play.

I started riding faster and was home in no time; I changed out of my good clothes, let King out of the chook-house and went back inside for a drink. I looked up and saw sitting in the glass cupboard, where Mum kept her treasures, a perfect lemon meringue pie. I didn't think she would notice if I ate some of the meringue, *if* I stayed near the edges. Before long however, I had eaten most of the topping and I groaned aloud; *"Ohhh no"* as I quickly tried to spread the bits that were left, over the top of the lemon. I wanted to get King and get us out of the back door quickly, before Mum came home, but she was walking in as we were running out.

Of course, she spotted her pie as soon as she put her purse on the shelf, and she told me it was the dessert for the visitors who were from her indoor bowling club. Mum said, "first impressions count," and she didn't think her visitors would be very impressed with the leftover pie. I had to go to the shop for ice-cream, and she would add that to the stewed fruit that was meant to be our dessert for dinner. After that I was allowed out to play, as long as I kept out of trouble, but I needed to come home after a couple of hours and meet the visitors. Somehow, luck was on my side, and I wasn't grounded, so King and I headed around the corner to see if any of the kids were out playing.

I could keep my "Sunday School only" watch on, as I needed to check the time. It was 11 a.m. now, and I had to be home by 1 p.m. to meet the visitors and have lunch. The watch had been a birthday present from my favourite uncle while he was overseas and was incredibly special. There were a few kids ready to play, so went over to the old church and decided it was a perfect afternoon to climb the trees. King was happily playing around us, and we had closed the gate, so he couldn't escape. After climbing up and looking down on the cemetery for a while, we decided we would go and play on the playground, before we went home for lunch.

We were having a wonderful time and then I remembered I needed to be home by 1:00 so I looked at my watch, but it wasn't on my wrist. I couldn't believe it and looked under the swings and see-saws and in the grass around the playground, but I couldn't see my watch anywhere. When I got home, it was after 1:00pm and then I had to explain that I had lost my watch somewhere. I had that awful gut feeling again.

Mum said I had to re-trace my steps in my memory and think of where I had been. I decided it would be quicker to pray to God to help me, and then I remembered the trees. I ran back to the old church and rushed up the first tree I had climbed. I had to slide over the roof and climb down another tree, and then I saw my little watch, hanging safely from one of the branches. I breathed a great big sigh of relief and whispered "thank you".....

The visitors didn't seem to know they weren't getting the dessert they should have, and they were all happily chatting. We were going to have bread, honey, and cream for dessert, plus we could have the rest of the lemon meringue pie. We were allowed to go to the shop and buy a soft drink each. I bought fizzy cola and I put it in the fridge until after dinner then went off to play with my friends again. We decided to visit Heather and keep her company for a while. Her Mum was home, so we just hung around in the front yard; I don't think she wanted us to take Heather anywhere. Heather said her Mum wasn't too impressed when she came home with her plaster a bit damp, and the drawings all smudged.

After a while it was time to head home again, and we all went in our own directions. I put King in with the chooks and went inside to get my fizzy cola from the fridge. I opened it with the bottle opener and took a big drink, which I had to spit out, because it was cold tea. My brother had sneakily opened the lid, tipped my drink into another container, and re-filled the bottle with cold tea. Of course, my fizzy drink no longer had any fizz, and he thought that was so funny he nearly fell over laughing, but I didn't think it was funny at all. He said he was paying me back because we were not having our fruit for dessert because I had ruined the pie, and we were stuck with bread and honey and cream instead.

More words of "Sing a Song of Sixpence" popped into my mind "The king was in his counting house counting out his money; the queen was in the parlor eating bread and honey" and I thought there was nothing wrong with eating bread and honey anyway.

Chapter 8 – Tadpoles and Frogs

Here it was, Monday morning of the second week of our holidays already. I knew I had to make extra pocket money to help pay for things King needed, so I decided to make some toffees to sell to the neighbours. I found the recipe I had seen Mum use, and knew it was easy to boil the mixture, so I just had to follow the instructions and stir until cooked. That went well, but I had a great idea on how to save time; I would pour the cooked toffee into the ice block container and put it into the freezer to set quicker, and I wouldn't need to use the little patty pans.

"Oh no!" That was not such a clever idea at all because the ice block container didn't like the hot toffee and the toffee melted the bottom of each section, and there was hot toffee running everywhere. I had to boil the kettle and run the water over the gooey mess, and once I had cleaned it up, I made a new batch, but this time I poured the hot toffee mix into the little patty cake pans.

Once the toffees had cooled down a bit, I placed them on a flat tray and put them into the freezer and thought I would sell them later that afternoon. I didn't think there would be much money left over though as there was the ice block container to replace, and I thought I should give Mum some money for the ingredients I had used for the toffees. I had made a few mistakes lately and Mum said she couldn't wait for school to start again. I sort of laughed to myself because there were still 7 weeks to go!

When everything was back in order, the toffees in the freezer and the chores done, I took King to our meeting place and there was seven of us ready to start today's fun and plan what we would get up to. Although I didn't have any special shampoo for King yet, I had used my brush and brushed him until he looked perfect and very handsome. He really was a King! Well, at least to me, anyway.

We decided to get our bikes and ride to visit Heather again as she still couldn't ride her bike with her cast on. Her Mum worked as well, so we decided to play in the playground near her place, and King was having fun, running here and there, sniffing all the new scents of the other kids and animals. He was so well behaved, it didn't matter if another dog or cat came into sight, he never ran off and just stayed with us. My heart grew so big with love for him that it almost hurt. I was sure God had heard my prayers and that He could see how much I loved and cared for King. Maybe his old owners had moved a long way away and couldn't get back to find King.

There was a huge slippery dip at this playground, with bigger teeter-totters and swings and a hurdy gurdy that swung us right out until we were nearly sideways as we were swinging. There was also a witch's hat that we stood on as someone swung us around and around. Heather couldn't really play, but she seemed to be happy having King sitting next to her when he wasn't running around, and at least she wasn't sitting inside, when all this glorious sunshine was here for us to enjoy.

Of course, we all started to get hungry, and we headed to our own homes for lunch. I thought I would boil an egg and was sure I knew what I was doing as Mum had made them often enough. I put the saucepan on the stove, with an egg and water covering it and waited for it to boil. While I was waiting, I checked the toffees and for some reason, they were still very gooey and had pushed the little patty pans right out of shape, so the toffee was leaking over the edges and onto the tray. Surely everything froze in the freezer!

I decided to leave them there a bit longer, and the water for my egg was boiling so time to take it out. When I cracked the egg open, it was also runny and gooey, and I really couldn't eat it at all. What had happened to the egg? Maybe I should just stay out of the kitchen and the laundry and leave things to my elder sister and Mum to sort out. I didn't toss the egg into the bin but mixed it in with King's dog food as I thought the egg would be good for him. He lapped it up and looked like he really enjoyed it, so at least I hadn't wasted the egg, although I had wasted the first toffee mix, which I helped go down the drain.

After washing up the few dishes I had made, I took King and decided to walk around the corner and see if the little dancing twins wanted to take him for a little walk on the footpath. They were so cute but a bit young to play with us when we rode our bikes, so we went to their home, and they were very happy to take King for a little walk. The smiles on their faces made me feel happy too. Life was so good, even though some things I was trying to do were not really going to plan.

King and I left Rachael and Hilary to meet up with a few of our other friends and decided to go and look for some tadpoles, although we didn't go into the drain again. We didn't want to leave King behind, and we didn't think he would enjoy the drain after what he had been through, so we went to the little swampy stream which was close. John and Rodney brought their home-made strainer and the jar with the holes in the lid, and after a while, we all had at least two tadpoles each that we could take home, and watch turn into frogs. At school, the teacher had told us this was known as a metamorphosis, and that was a very impressive name.

We left the little swamp then and each went home to settle our tadpoles into the containers we set up for them. I used an old ice-cream container and added a few rocks ready for when they got their back legs. Enough little insects would fly around the container for them to eat, so now all I had to do was wait until their little back legs started to grow and their tails fell off, then their little front legs would be growing as well. King was a bit curious but didn't drink the water and swallow the tadpoles, so I could leave the container under the bush near the back tap, where they would be in the shade and out of the hot afternoon sun and still get the early morning sun.

Chapter 9 – King is now a Prince

Mum would be home soon, and so would my brother and sisters, so I took King inside and we watched the cartoons on the TV. Well, King didn't really watch the TV, but he loved lying next to me with his head on my lap, and I just patted him the whole time. If I stopped patting him, he would get his paw and push my arm, telling me to start patting him again. He was so clever! Mum came home first, and as usual, she brought the paper home with her as she like to read it all but enjoyed doing the crossword.

She must have gone straight to the lost and found section because next thing, she told me there was an ad in the paper for a lost golden Labrador, and my heart dropped. The lost dog belonged to a little boy with disabilities, and there was a phone number and a reward for anyone who knew where the dog was. My heart really sank as Mum rang the number and the lady that answered told her that his name was Prince. Mum called out "Prince" and King's beautiful head flew up with excitement – there was no doubt my King was now a Prince.

The family were so excited that they had found their Prince they wanted to come over straight away and pick him up. They didn't live that far, and before long, the car pulled up out the front and the little boy's parents helped from the car and Prince went flying over to him, licking him all over. Then Prince/King came running back over to me, licking me all over and he started running between the little boy and back to me, like he was unsure about saying goodbye. I was crying so much I could hardly see what was going on and didn't want to take the reward money they were offering, so they gave it to my Mum, and she held onto it.

We stayed out the front and I watched them drive off with my King, and my heart felt like it had sunk to my feet. I went into my room and lay down on my bed, crying and feeling sorry for myself and asking God why didn't He hear my prayers and why didn't He see how much I loved King?

I wasn't hungry and didn't get up again after that, and the next morning, I didn't bother getting up early and didn't join the others with whatever plans they made for the day. My heart was breaking and without King the home seemed so empty. Even Max knew something was wrong as he wasn't strutting around like he would normally, and Ethyl and Alice were just cuddling up to each other in one of the roosting boxes. I could see Mum had put the reward money in the cupboard with the glass doors, but I left it there as I really felt guilty taking it at all. How could I have a reward for loving King?

All I did that day was mope around the house, and laid on my bed, still crying tears that somehow hurt my throat. No more walks with the little dancing twins, no more King running around while we were at the playground and no more excited licks and greetings when I came home after being away for a little while. No more beautiful head laying on my lap or a little paw pushing me to continue patting him. Oh God, how can I carry on?

Chapter 10 – My Prayers are answered

Mum came home from work and my brother and sisters were home too, and I could see they felt sorry for me as they all knew how much I loved King. Somehow though, Mum seemed to be a bit excited, which didn't make sense to me at all. We had special pancakes that night, and they were light and usually easy to swallow but my throat struggled to swallow the food. We also had ice cream for dessert and that somehow helped my throat, and it didn't seem as sore as it was.

Mum had seen the toffees I had made to make some pocket money to help with King when she got the ice cream from the freezer. She told me toffees aren't set in the freezer and that I hadn't cooked the mixture long enough to set. Mum told me she would teach me how to make toffees soon and I could still earn some pocket money to spend how I wanted. I did have to scrape the toffee mixture onto some paper and clean the freezer with hot soapy water. I'm not sure that I thought making more toffees was such a good idea, but with Mum's help, I knew they would be perfect.

After we had cleared up, we sat in the loungeroom to watch TV, and there was a knock at the door. Mum jumped up and went to open the door, but I just sat where I was as I wasn't interested in visitors. When I heard the voices, they reminded me of the people who had come and picked up their Prince. I looked through the window and sure enough, there was the car with the little boy sitting in the back seat. I had to go to the door to check out what was going on, and lo and behold, they had a little golden Labrador puppy, wiggling in the lady's arms.

They had been surprised at how much their Prince had learned to love me in such a short time, as he kept running back to me and then back to the little boy who loved him so much. They handed me the puppy and asked me if I wanted him, and I looked at Mum and she said "YES" it was okay for this little puppy to be mine.

Without me knowing, they had planned with my mother to sell us the little puppy with the reward money that I hadn't wanted. They had ordered the little puppy when they had lost their Prince, because the little boy depended on having a dog to love and cherish.

I ran to the cupboard and got the reward money from where Mum had left it, and gave them the money, and I felt like I was in Heaven. Of course, I named him King. He had a collar and a little lead on already, but he hadn't been trained at all. When I put him on the ground, he was pulling away from me, and I laughed out loud, knowing there would be so much fun, filled with a lot of love to come, training this little puppy.

Oh, thank you God; you did hear my prayers!

Acknowledgements: -

Illustrations: – Next Mars Media

Songs mentioned: -

The Wise Man Built His House Upon the Rocks
Old Macdonald Had a Farm
The Grand Old Duke of York
Sing a Song of Sixpence
Jesus Loves the Little Children
There was an Old Man Named Michael Finnegan
On Top of Spaghetti (all covered in cheese)

Other books in this series: -

Training a King
Fun with Fury
Queen Puggy

ANGELS IN FLIGHT